Quick Group Devotions for Children's Ministry

Group
Books

Loveland, Colorado

List of Contributors

Esther Bailey
Karen Ball
Kim Egolf-Fox
Dean Feldmeyer
Mike Gillespie
Cindy Hansen
Bob Hicks
Delores Johnson
Janet Kageler
Sue McCallum

Scott McKee
Ed McNulty
Derrick Mueller
Jeffrey Nelson
Jolene Roehlkepartain
Linda Snyder
Norman Stolpe
Terry Vermillion
Carol Younger
Chris Yount

Quick Group Devotions for Children's Ministry

Copyright © 1990 by Group Publishing, Inc.

Third Printing, 1992

Credits
Edited by Michael D. Warden
Designed by Judy Atwood Bienick
Cover design and illustrations by Jill Bendykowski

Scriptures quoted from *The Everyday Bible, New Century Version*, copyright © 1987, 1988 by Word Publishing, Dallas, Texas 75039. Used by permission.

Library of Congress Cataloging-in-Publication Data
Quick group devotions for children's ministry.
    p. cm.
    Summary: Fifty-two devotions for elementary school children on such topics as Christian faith, family, friends, and God.
    ISBN 1-55945-004-5
    1. Children—Prayer-books and devotions—English. 2. Church work with children. [1. Prayer books and devotions.] I. Group Books (Firm)
BV4571.2.Q85   1990
242'.62—dc20

90-34830
CIP
AC

Printed in the United States of America

Contents

Quick Devotions on Important Faith Subjects

Introduction

For years, finding quality Christian devotional materials for elementary children has been all but impossible. Sunday school teachers and other volunteers have had to constantly pull new ideas out of nowhere to keep kids interested and growing. At times, the grind can get frustrating. And not just for the leaders. Children need active, quality programming that relates the Bible to their lives in ways they can understand.

Finally, an answer!

Quick Group Devotions for Children's Ministry is filled with devotions that can be used for junior church, after-school programs, Sunday school, vacation Bible school, day camps, children's time in a church service—and any other setting where children are gathered.

Devotion Elements

The creative devotions are based on a variety of scripture and a variety of themes. Each devotion consists of the following seven elements.

Theme: This is the devotion's topic, the main thought. Themes cover a variety of children's needs and concerns.

Scripture: Each devotion is based on scripture that supports the theme and shows kids that God is concerned about every area of their lives.

Overview: This brief statement describes the devotion and tells what the children will learn.

Preparation: This part describes exactly what materials you'll need for the devotion and what you'll need to do to prepare for it.

Experience: Each devotion contains a unique element that lets children actually experience the theme. Kids use their senses of sight, hearing, smell, touch and taste to help them understand the topic.

All activities can be adapted to fit your group's size. If you have a small group, simply do the devotional activities together. If your group is larger, divide into small groups. For example, you can divide into small groups by height or birthdays.

Response: Children take the experience one step further and think about what they've experienced and how it applies to their lives.

Closing: Each devotion concludes with a prayer or activity that summarizes the devotional thought and helps children apply it to their lives.

Be creative and have fun with *Quick Group Devotions for Children's Ministry*. Adapt and use these ready-to-go devotions wherever and whenever you want.

Quick Devotions on
GROWING CLOSER
TO GOD

★ A Good Beginning

By Cindy Hansen

★ **Theme:** New Year's

★ **Scripture:** Psalm 118:14 and Philippians 4:13

★ **Overview:** Children will run a quick relay, then write New Year's resolutions while munching cookies.

★ **Preparation:** For each person you'll need five Oreo cookies, a piece of paper and a pencil. You'll also need a Bible.

★ EXPERIENCE

Give kids each five Oreo cookies. Have children each stack their cookies in the palm of one of their hands. Form two teams, then have kids run a relay by each balancing their Oreo cookies in one hand while running to a line and back. Have runners start again if they drop a cookie.

After the relay, have children sit on the floor. Distribute a piece of paper and a pencil to each person. Let kids each eat one cookie while you explain that they're going to write New Year's resolutions.

Say: **A resolution is something you're going to try to start doing or improve on this year. Resolutions can deal with family, friends, school or church. For example, "I will help clean the kitchen after supper at least three times a week."**

Ask children each to write one resolution for each Oreo cookie in their hand.

★ RESPONSE

Have kids form Oreo trios by getting with two others sitting close by. Have them each share one resolution with their trio.

★ CLOSING

Read aloud Psalm 118:14 and Philippians 4:13.

Say: **God helps us with our resolutions. We don't have to change all by ourselves. He helps us to do the job.**

Close with Oreo cookie hugs. Have two children from each trio be the cookie "outsides" and have the remaining child be the cookie "insides." Have the outsides hug the insides. Have kids take turns being the insides so everyone is hugged.

Have children take the rest of the cookies home and eat them as reminders to keep their resolutions.

 Boo-Boos

By Terry Vermillion

★ *Theme:* Hurts

★ *Scripture:* Isaiah 40:28-31

★ *Overview:* Children receive adhesive bandages to show how God can make our hurts better.

★ *Preparation:* For each person you'll need a pen and a "Boo-boo strip"—an adhesive bandage with cartoon characters or designs on it. You'll also need a Bible.

★ EXPERIENCE

Form a circle.

Say: **We all get hurt sometimes. Maybe someone says something mean to us or we get overlooked when teams are picked at recess. Many times we don't share these hurts with our friends. But God knows what these hurts are. As friends in Christ we want to make the hurts better.**

Give children each a pen and have them each write on one palm a hurt they've had recently. Then read aloud Isaiah 40:28-31.

Ask: **What can your friends do to help heal your hurt? What can God do to heal your hurt? What can you do to help get over your hurt?**

★ RESPONSE

Give kids adhesive bandages and have them each put one on the hand of the person to their right, saying "God knows about your hurt."

★ CLOSING

Pray: **Dear God. Thanks for comforting us when we hurt. Help us to comfort each other. In Jesus' name, amen.**

Busy! Busy! Busy!

By Jolene Roehlkepartain

★ *Theme:* Busyness, stress

★ *Scripture:* Mark 6:45; Luke 5:15-16; and John 4:4-6

★ *Overview:* Children experience the stress of having too many balloons to juggle and discuss what to do about stress.

★ *Preparation:* You'll need three to four inflated balloons and a pen per person. You'll also need a Bible.

★ EXPERIENCE

Ask two volunteers to be balloon-poppers during the activity. Have the rest of the children hold hands, form a circle and then sit on the floor. Say: **The object is to keep hitting balloons without letting any balloons touch the floor.**

Start with one balloon. Gradually add more until there are too many balloons for the kids to handle. Have balloon-poppers stomp on any balloons that touch the ground.

★ RESPONSE

After a few minutes of balloons popping and kids trying to keep all the balloons in the air, stop the activity.

Ask: **What happened when there were too many balloons? How did you feel when balloons hit the floor? When do you feel like you have too many things to do?**

Read aloud Mark 6:45-46; Luke 5:15-16; and John 4:4-6.

Ask: **How did Jesus react when too much was going on in his life? Is it bad to say you need a break? Why or why not? What can we learn about stress and busyness from Jesus?**

★ CLOSING

Have children each pick up a shriveled-up, popped balloon. Give kids each a pen and have them each write on their balloon one thing that's causing them stress.

Pray: **God, forgive us when we mess up by trying to do too much. Help us to know when to slow down and when to come to you. Amen.**

After the prayer, have children each throw away their popped balloons to show how God takes care of their stress.

★ *Grumble! Grumble!*

By Mike Gillespie

★ ***Theme:*** Complaining

★ ***Scripture:*** Philippians 2:14-15

★ ***Overview:*** Children get tangled up in a clothesline to illustrate the bad effects of complaining.

★ ***Preparation:*** For each person you'll need a clothespin, a pencil and a piece of paper. You'll also need a Bible, scissors and a ball of string. String a clothesline across the room and attach the clothespins to it.

★ EXPERIENCE

Give kids each a pencil and a piece of paper. Have them each write on the paper everything they like to complain about. For example, "I like to complain about going to bed." Tell children each to pin their complaints on the clothesline.

When all complaints are pinned, have kids gather in a huddle. Wrap the clothesline around each person in the huddle until everyone is tangled up. Have children each sit on the floor.

Ask: **How does it feel to be wrapped up in all these complaints? How do complaints tie us down?**

★ RESPONSE

Read aloud Philippians 2:14-15.

Ask: **Why would the Bible tell us not to complain or grumble all the time? How do you feel when you're around someone who complains a lot?**

Say: **Complaining gets things all tied up just like we are right now. God wants us to learn to do things without complaining about them.**

★ CLOSING

Ask: **What's something from your list you want to stop complaining about?**

After kids respond, pray: **Dear God, help us stop**

complaining about so many things. Help us give up one of our complaints this week. In Jesus' name, amen.

As children leave, give them each a piece of string as a reminder of the activity.

★ *Hot Heads*

By Jolene Roehlkepartain

★ **Theme:** Anger

★ **Scripture:** Ephesians 4:26

★ **Overview:** Kids experience what happens when they stuff their angry feelings inside.

★ **Preparation:** For each person you'll need a canned soft drink. You'll also need a Bible.

★ EXPERIENCE

Play Hot Heads outside or in an area where you won't ruin carpet or furniture. Have children form a circle. Give one person a full, unopened can of soft drink.

Say: **When someone tosses you the can, shout one thing that makes you mad such as when Mom or Dad makes you clean your room or won't let you spend the night at a friend's house. Act fast to keep the can moving. When I yell "Stop and pop it open," the person holding the can must open it.**

On "go," have kids start tossing the can. After about three minutes, have kids speed up the game. After about another minute, yell: **Stop and pop it open!**

★ RESPONSE

Call everyone together and ask: **How did you feel when we started tossing the can faster and you knew someone had to open it? How is anger like the just-opened can?**

Read aloud Ephesians 4:26. Ask: **How can we handle our anger better? What should we do when we're angry?**

★ CLOSING

Give each person a canned soft drink. Then pray: **Thanks, God, for helping us with our anger. We know that when we talk about our anger right away we'll be less likely to blow up. So help us deal with our anger in a positive way, God. Thanks. In Jesus' name, amen.**

Never Fear

By Karen Ball

★ **Theme:** Fear

★ **Scripture:** Psalm 34:7

★ **Overview:** Kids provide a barrier of protection for one person, then discuss how God protects his children.

★ **Preparation:** You'll need a Bible.

★ EXPERIENCE

Ask for two volunteers. Have one stand in the center of the room, then have the rest of the group—except for the second volunteer—lock arms in a circle around the first volunteer to form a protective wall. Have the second volunteer try to get through the "wall" to the person in the middle while the rest of the group tries to keep the person protected.

★ RESPONSE

After a few minutes, have everyone sit on the floor.

Ask: **What was fun about this game? How was this like the way God protects us?**

Read aloud Psalm 34:7.

Ask: **How do you feel knowing you have angels all around you? How can we fight feelings of fear?**

★ CLOSING

Have children form a circle with arms around each other's shoulders.

Pray: **Dear God, thank you for sending your angels to protect us. Help us trust you, and teach us how to stop feelings of fear when they come. In Jesus' name, amen.**

★ Valentine, Be Mine

By Cindy Hansen

★ **Theme:** God's love

★ **Scripture:** John 3:16 and 1 John 4:16-19

★ **Overview:** Kids make valentines for each other and participate in a valentine prayer.

★ **Preparation:** For each person you'll need a marker, a construction paper heart and a candy heart with a message on it (available at grocery stores). You'll also need a Bible.

★ EXPERIENCE

Have children sit in a heart shape on the floor. Tell them this devotion will focus on hearts—ours and God's.

Give everyone a marker, a construction paper heart and a candy heart with a message on it. Have children each read their candy heart, then write a valentine's message on the construction paper heart using the phrase on their candy heart. For example, a valentine's message for "Wow" could be, "Wow! You're a neat person. Happy Valentine's Day."

★ RESPONSE

When children are finished, have them each give their construction paper heart to the person on their right. Let kids enjoy the candy. Have kids each share with the rest of the group the valentine they received.

Ask: **Why do we like to celebrate Valentine's Day? How is giving a valentine like sharing God's love? How can we share valentines all year long?**

★ CLOSING

Say: **On Valentine's Day we think of love. God loves us more than anyone else does. Here's how much he loves us.**

Read aloud John 3:16 and 1 John 4:16-19.

Close with a valentine prayer. Have kids stand and

join hands, still in the heart shape.

Say: **For the valentine prayer, I'll pause after saying each line. Each time I pause, you say "Be mine."**

Jesus loves us very much and says,

(Be mine.)

Through all your problems, he cares for you and says,

(Be mine.)

Through all your joys, he shares your happiness and says,

(Be mine.)

Jesus wants you to love others as he loves you. On Valentine's Day and every day he says,

(Be mine.)

Amen.

★*Phony? Phooey!*

By Ed McNulty

★ *Theme:* Making choices

★ *Scripture:* Isaiah 55:1-3

★ *Overview:* Kids handle real and artificial fruit to see how they must separate what's real from what's phony.

★ *Preparation:* For each person you'll need a piece of fruit. For every two people you'll need a piece of artificial fruit. You'll also need a bowl and a Bible. Set aside half of the real fruit, then put the rest of the real fruit and all of the artificial fruit in the bowl.

★ EXPERIENCE

Offer children each a piece of fruit from the bowl. Allow kids who have real fruit to eat, but have the rest of the group hold their phony fruit. Don't let kids with real fruit share their fruit.

★ RESPONSE

After about a minute, ask kids who have phony fruit: **How would it feel to try to eat a piece of phony fruit? Could you tell just by looking that it wasn't real? What purpose does the phony fruit serve?**

Ask the rest of the group: **How did it feel to get real fruit while others got phony fruit? Did you want to share your fruit? Why or why not?**

Say: **A long time ago God wanted his people to know the difference between the real and the phony in life. He sent Isaiah to help them.**

Read aloud Isaiah 55:1-3.

Say: **People sometimes choose phony things over real things in life. For example, some people want to be rich to bring happiness. But those are phony ways to happiness.**

Ask: **What are some other phony things people sometimes choose instead of real things?**

Tell kids that only God can help us choose the real over the phony in life.

★ CLOSING

Hold up some of the artificial fruit and pray: **Dear God, phony fruit is good to look at, but it can't satisfy our hunger. Help us to see that only our friendship with you and with each other is real and lasting. In Jesus' name, amen.**

Distribute the rest of the real fruit to kids who didn't get any earlier, then have everyone eat the fruit together as a reminder to choose real things over phony things.

★ Rubber Band Emotions

By Derrick Mueller

★ **Theme:** Emotions

★ **Scripture:** Ecclesiastes 3:1-8

★ **Overview:** Kids make faces using rubber bands, then discuss God's gift of emotions.

★ **Preparation:** You'll need a package of rubber bands and a Bible.

★ EXPERIENCE

Give each person several rubber bands. Have children each create different faces by stretching the rubber bands around their heads and faces. Challenge kids to use the rubber bands to imitate certain animals such as pigs or fish. Have kids each try to guess what animal each person is imitating. Finally, have kids each use the rubber bands to create a happy face, then a sad face. Applaud kids' efforts.

★ RESPONSE

Have children remove their rubber bands.

Then ask: **What makes you happy? What makes you sad? How do feelings help us? How can they hurt us?**

Read aloud Ecclesiastes 3:1-8.

Say: **There's nothing wrong with crying, being sad or laughing—God created all these feelings. There are times when you should feel sad and times when you should feel happy.**

Ask: **When is it okay to feel sad? happy? angry? afraid? When is it not appropriate to feel sad? happy? angry? afraid?**

★ CLOSING

Have kids each put one rubber band on their wrist to remind them that emotions are good when expressed in healthy ways.

Then pray: **Lord, thank you for creating us with emotions. We know there's a time for everything—including being sad, crying, laughing and being happy. Help us give our emotions to you so they can glorify you. In Jesus' name, amen.**

★*Surprise Package*

By Scott McKee

★ *Theme:* Holy Spirit

★ *Scripture:* 1 Corinthians 6:19

★ *Overview:* Children compare a secret hidden in a box to the Holy Spirit living in their hearts.

★ *Preparation:* For each person you'll need a 3x5 card and a pencil. You'll also need a Bible. Place a mirror in the bottom of a small box with an easy-open lid.

★ EXPERIENCE

Have children sit in a circle. Give them each a 3x5 card and a pencil. Hold up the box with a mirror.

Say: **This box contains a secret about God. I'm going to let each one of you look in it one at a time. When the box comes to you, peek inside but don't say anything. Write on your card what you think the secret is. Then pass the box to the next person.**

Give the box to one person in the circle.

★ RESPONSE

When everyone has finished, have children share what they've written. Then read aloud 1 Corinthians 6:19.

Ask: **According to this verse, where does the Holy Spirit live? If we're Christians, who do we belong to? How should the Holy Spirit living in us affect the way we live?**

★ CLOSING

Close with a circle prayer. Have children each pray for the person on their right by saying, "Lord, I thank you for (person's name). Please fill him or her with your Spirit."

Trusters and Trustees

By Norman Stolpe

★ **Theme:** Confidence

★ **Scripture:** Jeremiah 1:4-10

★ **Overview:** Children walk blindfolded on a 2×4, then discuss how to trust God to keep us safe when we do what he wants us to do.

★ **Preparation:** For every four kids, gather one 8- to 10-foot 2×4 and one blindfold. Space 2×4s each evenly as you lay them flat on the floor so adults can supervise for safety. You'll also need a Bible.

★ EXPERIENCE

Form pairs. Have pairs line up at one end of a 2×4. Blindfold one person in the first pair. Have blindfolded kids each walk the length of their 2×4 while holding their partner's hand. At the end of the 2×4, have partners trade roles and walk back. Pass the blindfold to the next pair and repeat the process. Continue until everyone has walked blindfolded.

★ RESPONSE

Have everyone sit in a circle. Ask children each to tell how their partner's guidance gave them confidence to walk the 2×4.

Read aloud Jeremiah 1:4-10.

Ask: **What made Jeremiah afraid? What kinds of things scare us? What did God do for Jeremiah's fear? How can we trust God to keep us from being afraid when we do what he wants us to do?**

★ CLOSING

Have everyone stand up and hold hands.

Pray: **Thanks, God, that you're just as close to each of us as the people we're holding hands with—even when we're afraid. Help us trust you to control what comes into our lives. In Jesus' name, amen.**

★ Undercover Lies

By Karen Ball

★ **Theme:** Honesty

★ **Scripture:** Proverbs 12:19

★ **Overview:** Kids try to hide rocks under a blanket to learn that you can't hide lies.

★ **Preparation:** For each person you'll need a fist-size rock. You'll also need a blanket and a Bible.

★ EXPERIENCE

Spread the blanket on the floor. Give children each a rock. Have them try to hide their rocks under the blanket so no bumps show. Then have kids remove the rocks and see how smooth they can make the blanket.

★ RESPONSE

Ask: **Why was it hard to conceal the rocks? How are these rocks like lies? Why do we tell lies? Why are lies so hard to hide?**

Read aloud Proverbs 12:19. Note how much easier it was to keep the blanket smooth when children weren't trying to hide something under it.

Ask: **Why would someone try to hide a lie? Why is it always best to be honest, even if it's hard?**

★ CLOSING

Have kids sit on the smoothed-out blanket.

Pray: **God, help us not to tell lies and then try to hide those lies. Help us be honest, even when it's hard. In Jesus' name, amen.**

★ *Undiluted Life*

By Delores Johnson

★ *Theme:* Self-control

★ *Scripture:* Colossians 3:5-10

★ *Overview:* By diluting concentrated orange juice, kids see how a lack of self-control dilutes the quality of life.

★ *Preparation:* For each person you'll need a cup. You'll also need two cans of concentrated orange juice, a punch bowl, a spoon, a Bible and plenty of water.

★ EXPERIENCE

Empty one can of concentrated orange juice into the punch bowl. Read aloud Colossians 3:5-10. As you read, have a volunteer pour in one can of water for each sin mentioned. Stir the mixture, then give children each a cup and have them taste the diluted orange juice.

Ask: **What's wrong with this orange juice? How is this orange juice like what happens when we let sin in our lives?**

★ RESPONSE

Say: **When we let sin come into our lives, our hearts become "watered-down" and tasteless, and we lose God's peace and joy.**

Prepare the second can of orange juice correctly. Have children each taste this orange juice.

Ask: **How is this undiluted orange juice like having self-control? Why is it better to keep sin out of our lives? How does God reward those who obey him?**

★ CLOSING

Ask: **What's the difference between the two orange juices? Which was better? Why?**

Pray: **God, help us turn away from sin and be self-controlled. Continue to fill us with your life. In Jesus' name, amen.**

★ *Worry War*

By Karen Ball

★ **Theme:** Worry

★ **Scripture:** Matthew 13:22 and Philippians 4:6-7

★ **Overview:** Group members write worries on rocks, then see how holding onto worries can weigh them down.

★ **Preparation:** For each person you'll need a piece of chalk. You'll also need a bucket full of fist-size rocks and a Bible. Make sure you have enough rocks so each person can have one.

★ EXPERIENCE

Place the bucket full of rocks in the center of the room. Give children each a piece of chalk. Have them each get a rock from the bucket and write on their rock one thing that worries them. Then have kids each say their worry as they each put their rock in the bucket. Have a few kids each try to lift the bucket alone. Give kids each someone else's "worry." Empty out any remaining rocks, then have someone who couldn't lift the full bucket lift the empty bucket.

★ RESPONSE

Read aloud Matthew 13:22 and Philippians 4:6-7.

Ask: **What kinds of things worry us? How can worry hurt us? How are these rocks like worries?**

Say: **Just like carrying lots of rocks is hard, so carrying lots of worries can weigh us down.**

Ask: **How does sharing our worries with others and with God make them easier to handle?**

★ CLOSING

Have kids each take home the rock you gave them and pray for that person's concern or worry.

Pray: **God, we want to let go of our worries. Help us to**

tell you and our friends about what's worrying us and then to let go of those worries. Thank you that you care about us and will take care of us. In Jesus' name, amen.

Quick Devotions on
GETTING ALONG
WITH OTHERS

A Strong Body

By Dean Feldmeyer

Theme: Unity

Scripture: 1 Corinthians 12:27

Overview: By breaking apart threads, children learn that Christians are strong when they stand together.

Preparation: You'll need lots of foot-long pieces of thread and a Bible.

EXPERIENCE

Distribute the thread to the children—one piece to the first person, two pieces to the second person, three to the third, and so on throughout the group.

Starting with the first person, invite children each to break the thread using their hands. Kids holding bundles of threads must break them all at the same time.

Stop whenever someone can't break his or her threads. Take away that person's threads—one at a time—until he or she can break the bundle.

RESPONSE

After everyone has broken his or her threads, ask: **Why is it easy to break one or two threads but difficult to break a whole bunch?**

Read aloud 1 Corinthians 12:27.

Say: **Paul says that even though we're all different, we're all part of the same body—like a human body.**

Ask: **What happens to the body if it loses a part? What if we lose a part that seems unimportant, such as a pinky finger?**

Ask kids to imagine the threads are members of the group.

Ask: **How do we make the group strong? How could we make it weak?**

CLOSING

Pray for children who're absent today, asking God to

build the kids into one strong body and to help them
realize they're weaker when they aren't united.

Easter Feaster

By Cindy Hansen

Theme: Easter

Scripture: Matthew 5:13; Luke 24:1-8; and John 6:35

Overview: Group members prepare a submarine sandwich, read Bible verses and think about Jesus' Resurrection.

Preparation: You'll need a 3-foot loaf of French bread, a knife, mustard, mayonnaise, assorted meats and cheeses, lettuce, tomatoes, fruit, utensils, napkins, cups, drinks and a Bible. For each person you'll need a few pieces of Easter candy.

EXPERIENCE

Say: **When Easter comes we think of God's great gift of Jesus. We think of Jesus' life and all the things he taught us. Today we're going to read some Bible verses on these thoughts and prepare a submarine sandwich as we go.**

Give a couple of children the bread and a knife. Read aloud John 6:35 as they cut the bread in half—lengthwise.

Ask: **What does Jesus mean when he says he's the bread of life? Why do we need him to live a good life?**

Give a couple of kids the mustard and mayonnaise to spread on the bread. Have two others add meat and cheese on top. Read aloud Matthew 5:13.

Ask: **What would this sandwich taste like without salt in the meat or without mustard or mayonnaise to season it? What would we be like as Christians if we were "saltless"?**

Ask a couple of other kids to top off the sandwich by adding lettuce and tomatoes. When they're done, have them cut a sandwich section for each person. Set aside the sandwiches until the end.

RESPONSE

Ask children to think silently about Jesus' life, Death

and Resurrection while you read aloud Luke 24:1-8. Have them each think of one thing they thank Jesus for. After a few seconds, have kids join hands.

Then start a prayer by saying: **Thanks, Jesus, for living for us and giving us an example. Thanks for dying for us and taking our sins on you. Thanks for rising on Easter to give us eternal life. Hear our thoughts of other things we're thankful for . . .**

Have kids each say one thing they're thankful for. When everyone has prayed, have kids say in unison, "Amen."

 # CLOSING

Distribute the sandwich sections. Add other goodies such as milk or pop and fruit. For dessert, indulge in a few pieces of Easter candy. Happy Easter Feast!

Basic Training

By Kim Egolf-Fox

Theme: Helping each other

Scripture: Romans 1:12

Overview: Children receive back rubs—something they can't do for themselves—then talk about why they need each other.

Preparation: You'll need a Bible.

EXPERIENCE

Have kids each try to give themselves a back rub. After about a minute of trying, have children form a tight circle. Then have them each turn to the right.

Say: **Place your hands on the person's back in front of you and give him or her a back rub.**

After about a minute, say: **Now turn around and give the person in front of you a back rub.**

Allow about another minute. Then have kids sit down in a circle.

RESPONSE

Ask: **What was it like to get back rubs from others? How is it different when you try to give yourself a back rub? Besides a back rub, what are some things you can't do by yourself?**

Read aloud Romans 1:12.

Say: **Just as you can't give yourself a back rub, neither can you be a Christian alone. God gives us each other so we can help each other.**

CLOSING

One at a time, have children each take hold of the person's hand to their right and say, "I give you my hand because you're part of God's family." When everyone's holding hands, have kids lift their neighbors' hands high in the air and yell, "Amen!"

🍎 Family Friction

By Jolene Roehlkepartain

🍎 **Theme:** Family tensions
🍎 **Scripture:** Matthew 18:15
🍎 **Overview:** Kids experience friction and learn the importance of dealing with it right away.
🍎 **Preparation:** You'll need a Bible.

🍎 EXPERIENCE

Form pairs. Within each pair, have partners figure out which person has the most red on. Have all the "reddest" children leave the room with the leader.

Outside of the room, tell children each to ask questions about their partner's week, such as: What did you do this week? What fun activity did you do? What dull activity did you do? Tell kids to yawn openly each time their partner talks.

Say: **Keep yawning until your partner tells you it bugs him or her and that you should stop.**

Have children each go back into the room and start asking their partners questions. Let kids annoy their partners until several people tell their partner to stop.

🍎 RESPONSE

Bring the group together.

Ask: **How did you feel when your partner kept yawning? How long did it take to tell your partner that it annoyed you? What things do your family members do that annoy you?**

Read aloud Matthew 18:15.

Ask: **How often do you tell people in your family when they do something that bothers you? Why don't you tell them? How would it help if you did?**

🍎 CLOSING

Have children form a circle and hold hands. Have the group do one big yawn at the same time.

Then pray: **God, we sometimes annoy the people we live with. And they sometimes annoy us. Help us to be honest and say when something bothers us. When friction happens, help us work things out by being honest. Thank you for our families. In Jesus' name, amen.**

Friendship Vision

By Dean Feldmeyer

Theme: Friends

Scripture: Luke 15:20

Overview: By creating a visual illusion, children learn that their friends see them the way they really are—and love them anyway.

Preparation: For each person you'll need a piece of paper. You'll also need a Bible.

EXPERIENCE

Distribute paper. Give children these instructions:

1. **Roll the paper into a tube about an inch in diameter. Look through it with your right eye. Close your left eye.**

2. **Now hold your left hand up beside the tube, with your palm toward your face and your little finger touching the side of the tube.**

3. **Open both eyes. What do you see?**

Kids should see a hole in their left hand. After each

Tube Illusion

child has experienced the illusion, collect the papers.

● RESPONSE

Ask: **How did you get a hole in your left hand? How did it heal so quickly? Was there really a hole in your hand?**

Say: **Sometimes people are like this. We see them one way but they're really another way. If we like a person we may see him or her as attractive. If we don't like people we may see them as unattractive.**

But sometimes we aren't seeing people the way they really are. Sometimes they're different from the way we see them because they're putting on an act or because something is messing up our vision—like the tube.

● CLOSING

Read aloud Luke 15:20.

Say: **Here, the father saw his son the way he really was and still loved him. Friends are like this—they see us the way we really are, and they love us anyway.**

Close with a prayer thanking God for friends who see us the way we really are and who love us just the way we are.

🍎 *Feeling Wormy*

By Kim Egolf-Fox

🍎 **Theme:** Being left out, feeling low

🍎 **Scripture:** Psalm 22:1-8, 23-24

🍎 **Overview:** Kids experience what it feels like to be ignored, then hear that God doesn't leave people out.

🍎 **Preparation:** You'll need a Bible.

🍎 EXPERIENCE

Form groups of five or fewer. Have the person in each group wearing the most white be "It." Have kids start talking together, but totally ignore "It." Tell "It" to do whatever he or she can—short of physical touch—to be noticed by others.

After about one minute, have children sit in a circle. Ask the "Its": **How did you feel being left out? What did you do to be noticed?**

Ask the others: **How did you feel during the exercise? Why?**

🍎 RESPONSE

Read aloud Psalm 22:1-8.

Say: **This Psalm shows us the pain of a person who felt abandoned even by God.**

Read aloud Psalm 22:23-24.

Ask: **What in these last verses makes you think this person believed God still cared about him?**

🍎 CLOSING

Say: **We know from this Psalm that God still cares for us even when we feel left out. God doesn't leave people out.**

Pray: **Thank you, God, for not turning away from us when we feel left out. In Jesus' name, amen.**

Have children huddle together and give each other a big group hug.

Friends Forever

By Dean Feldmeyer

● **Theme:** Supporting friends
● **Scripture:** Proverbs 17:17
● **Overview:** By supporting each other physically, children learn what it means to support each other in friendship.
● **Preparation:** You'll need a Bible.

● EXPERIENCE

Form pairs. Have kids stand back to back with their partners and lock elbows. Then have kids each lean back and step forward so they're leaning against their partner

Partner Positions

to keep them from falling.

RESPONSE

Have kids each sit on the floor. Read aloud Proverbs 17:17. Say: **According to this verse, friends care about each other at all times, not just when things go well.**

Ask: **How is friendship like leaning on each other? How can we lean on each other so we don't fall when times are tough?**

Invite kids to share a time they leaned on a friend when they needed support or when a friend leaned on them.

CLOSING

Thank God for giving us true friends who stick with us even when times are hard. Ask God to help us be better friends—to be strong for others so they can lean on us when they need support.

 Friend Sticks

By Terry Vermillion

 Theme: Friendship

 Scripture: Romans 12:17-18

 Overview: Children make stick puppets of themselves and a friend, and focus on how they can be better friends.

 Preparation: For each person you'll need two tongue depressors and a bottle of glue. You'll also need an assortment of felt scraps, goggle eyes, yarn scraps and markers.

EXPERIENCE

Give kids each two tongue depressors and a bottle of glue, and have them each create two stick puppets using the supplies. Have children each make one puppet to represent themselves and another to represent a friend.

When puppets are finished, gather kids in a circle and tell them to look at their puppets and pretend that the two friends are meeting. Have children each imagine what the friends say to each other.

Ask: **Do you think your friend is happy with the way you treat him or her? Do you want to change anything about how you treat your friend?**

RESPONSE

Read aloud Romans 12:17-18.

Ask volunteers to say how they felt when they pretended to be their friend.

Ask: **Does your friend think you are a kind and caring person? Is there anything your friend wants you to change?**

CLOSING

Pray: **God help us treat our friends the way we want to be treated. In Jesus' name, amen.**

Have kids take their puppets home as reminders to be good friends to others.

Helping Hands

By Esther Bailey

Theme: Compassion

Scripture: 1 John 3:17-18

Overview: By sharing a treat with someone whose hands are tied, children learn to be more sensitive to others' needs.

Preparation: For each person you'll need a cookie or piece of candy. For every two people you'll need a 2-foot cord of yarn. You'll also need a Bible.

EXPERIENCE

Form pairs and give each pair a cord of yarn. Have the older child in each pair use his or her yarn to tie the younger child's hands behind his or her back. Give two cookies or two pieces of candy to each older partner. Watch as children get the idea of feeding their partners. When pairs finish eating, have older children each untie their partner's hands.

RESPONSE

Call everyone together and ask: **If your hands were tied, how did you feel when your hands were tied and the treats were passed out? If your hands were free, how did you feel when you had two goodies and your partner had none?**

Read aloud 1 John 3:17-18.

Ask: **Can you think of a time when you knew about someone who really needed help? Was there anything you could do to help?**

CLOSING

Have partners face each other, join both hands and bow their heads as you pray: **Dear Lord, help us to feel the pain when others are hurting. When we find someone whose hands are tied by misfortune, help us to be the hands of Jesus in showing love. In Jesus' name, amen.**

🍎 Helping Out

By Dean Feldmeyer

🍎 **Theme:** Helping each other
🍎 **Scripture:** Galatians 6:2
🍎 **Overview:** By locking fingers with another person and trying to pull them apart, children learn that we're stronger when we pull together.
🍎 **Preparation:** You'll need a Bible.

🍎 EXPERIENCE

Form pairs. Have partners each stand face to face and lock one finger with each other. Then have pairs each pull until the lock is broken.

Say: **Easy, huh? Now—using one hand—lock two fingers together and pull them apart.**

After pairs finish, say: **A little harder. Now lock three fingers together and pull them apart.**

Continue until pairs each clasp hands (lock all five fingers) and try to pull them apart.

🍎 RESPONSE

Read aloud Galatians 6:2.

Ask: **Why is it important for Christians to help each other?**

Have volunteers share when someone has helped them or when they've helped another person.

Ask: **What did it feel like to be helped? to help?**

🍎 CLOSING

Have kids each hold up each finger in succession while repeating the following after you:

(One finger)
God makes each of us strong.
(Two fingers)
But two Christians are stronger than one.
(Three fingers)
Three Christians can provide more help than two.

(Four fingers)
And if we keep adding more Christians to our group,
(Five fingers)
we become strong enough to help each other as well as other people. And if we do that . . .
(Make a fist.)
we can change the world.

🍎 Off-White Lies

By Mike Gillespie

🍎 **Theme:** Telling lies

🍎 **Scripture:** Ephesians 4:25

🍎 **Overview:** Kids play a game to separate true and false statements about others, then talk about how lies hurt relationships.

🍎 **Preparation:** You'll need a 1-pound bag of M&M's and a Bible.

🍎 EXPERIENCE

Ask kids each to think of two facts about themselves. Have them think of facts others don't know, such as "When I was 3 years old I broke my arm." Then have kids each think of one convincing lie to go along with the two facts. Have kids each share their two facts and one lie—without saying which is which. After each person shares, have the group vote on which statement is the lie. Give three M&M's to each person who correctly identifies the lie. Repeat the process for each person, awarding three M&M's for every correct vote. The person with the most M&M's at the end of the game wins.

🍎 RESPONSE

Read aloud Ephesians 4:25.

Ask: **Why does Paul tell us not to lie to each other? How do you feel when someone lies to you? When was a time you were hurt by a lie?**

Say: **Lies hurt and destroy relationships. Being a follower of Jesus means we don't lie.**

🍎 CLOSING

Pray together: **Dear God, help us be brave and tell the truth. Comfort us when we get hurt by a lie. Teach us that Jesus wants his followers to tell the truth. In Jesus' name, amen.**

Have kids each join hands and repeat the following

pledge after you. Pause after each line. Say:

We belong to Jesus.
Because we belong to Jesus,
we belong to each other.
We'll tell each other the truth.
And be Christlike toward others.

Shoebox Sharing

By Jolene Roehlkepartain

● **Theme:** Sharing lives

● **Scripture:** Hebrews 4:13

● **Overview:** Children get to know each other better and learn that God knows everything about them.

● **Preparation:** For each person you'll need a piece of paper and a pencil. Ask kids each to bring a shoebox with three or four items that represent their hobbies and interests. You'll also need a marker and a Bible.

● EXPERIENCE

Have kids each bring a shoebox with three or four items inside that represent their interests. Number the boxes. Don't allow kids to see whose box is whose.

Have kids sit in a circle. Display all the boxes with lids open on the floor in the center. Give children each a piece of paper and a pencil. Have kids each write their guesses of which shoebox belongs to which person. See who gets the most correct.

● RESPONSE

After kids guess which box belongs to which person, have children each retrieve their own box and explain what's in it.

Then ask: **How much did you learn about people in the room? Why? How can we learn more about each person?**

Read aloud Hebrews 4:13.

Ask: **How well does God know us? Why is it good for God to know so much about us? Why is it good for us to know a lot about each other?**

● CLOSING

Have kids each put their shoebox in the middle. Then have children hold hands and form a circle. Do a one-word, open-eye prayer. Going around the circle, have kids each thank God for one thing they see in a shoebox or for one person in the circle.

 Sibling Ties

By Dean Feldmeyer

Theme: Siblings

Scripture: Genesis 4:9

Overview: By being bound together, kids learn that being responsible for others requires cooperation.

Preparation: For every two people you'll need a 2-foot piece of string. You'll also need scissors and a Bible.

EXPERIENCE

Form pairs. Have children each use the string to join one wrist with their partner's opposite wrist. Let kids do this on their own.

Once pairs are tied together, give them each a task to accomplish; for example, straighten chairs, pick up litter, move furniture or hand out books. When the tasks are accomplished, gather kids in a circle and collect the strings.

Ask: **How is being tied together like having a brother or sister? What ties brothers and sisters together?**

RESPONSE

Read aloud Genesis 4:9.

Say: **In this story, one brother asks God, "Is it my job to take care of my brother?"**

Ask: **What does it mean to take care of a brother or sister? Why should we take care of our brothers and sisters?**

Say: **Siblings—brothers and sisters—are tied together by family ties like the string we used. Sometimes this is nice, and sometimes it's a pain. When we're tied to someone—by string or by family—everything's a lot simpler if we cooperate.**

CLOSING

Have children each share what it was like to do a task while tied to someone.

Ask: **What was hard about working while tied to someone? How could watching out for each other make it easier? How can we start taking better care of our brothers and sisters at home?**

Close with prayer, asking God to help kids care for their siblings.

Tear Yourself Away

By Linda Snyder

● **Theme:** Peer pressure

● **Scripture:** 1 Peter 2:11-12

● **Overview:** Children experience the difficulty of "tearing away" from peer pressure by joining in a paper-tearing game.

● **Preparation:** For each person you'll need four pieces of paper and a pencil. You'll also need a Bible.

● EXPERIENCE

Give each person four pieces of paper and a pencil.

Say: **Sometimes our friends pressure us to do things we don't really want to do. If only one or two people pressure us it may be easy to say no. But when everyone does it, it's hard not to give in. On one piece of your paper, write something your friends have pressured you to do. Then fold your paper in half. Pretend the fold represents one person saying, "Do it. No one will ever know!"**

After children have folded their papers, say: **Try to tear your paper in two.**

Then ask: **Why wasn't it hard to tear the paper? Is it hard to say no to just one person? Why or why not?**

Repeat the process two more times—each time with a fresh piece of paper. Once have kids each fold their paper twice. Then have kids each fold their paper five times. Repeat the questions, noting how the paper gets harder to tear the more times it's folded.

● RESPONSE

Ask: **How are the folds in this paper like peer pressure? Why is it harder to say no to several friends than it is to say no to just one?**

Read aloud 1 Peter 2:11-12.

Say: **Jesus wants us to throw off or tear away from everything that can tangle us up in sin. He died on the cross so we would be able to do what's right. With Jesus' help, we can always say no to negative peer pressure.**

CLOSING

On their last piece of paper, have kids each write "Jesus," then fold their paper five times. Have kids each take their paper home to remind them that Jesus' love is stronger than peer pressure.

Pray: **Dear Lord, when friends pressure us to sin, help us look to you for strength. You alone can help us tear away from anything that's sinful. In Jesus' name, amen**

 The Big Surprise

By Mike Gillespie

Theme: Showing love

Scripture: 1 Corinthians 10:31

Overview: Children receive an object to share with someone in the coming week as a way to express God's love.

Preparation: For each person you'll need a simple gift; for example, a fast-food coupon, candy bar, happy-face sign or chewing gum. Put the gifts in a paper sack. You'll also need a Bible.

EXPERIENCE

Have kids sit in a circle and close their eyes. Then pass around the sack and let kids each pick out the first item they touch.

When everyone has a gift, ask: **How can you use this item this week to share God's love with someone?**

RESPONSE

Read aloud 1 Corinthians 10:31.

Ask: **How do you react when you get a surprise you don't expect? How does it feel to give away something to someone else? How does giving please God?**

CLOSING

Pray: **Dear God, help us each share our gift with someone this week. Use us to bring a surprise to others that will let them know they're loved. In Jesus' name, amen.**

❤ The Tie That Binds

By Jeffrey Nelson

❤ **Theme:** Cooperation
❤ **Scripture:** Acts 2:46-47
❤ **Overview:** Kids hold on to a rope circle and lean back to discover what they can do by working together.
❤ **Preparation:** You'll need a 25-foot rope and a Bible.

❤ EXPERIENCE

Tie the rope into a circle about the size made by the children when they stand in a circle. Lay the rope in the middle of your group. Have kids each grab the rope with both hands and pull it so it's fully stretched. Then challenge them to slowly lean backward as far as they dare.

Repeat the process—each time with fewer people—to see at what point the task becomes too hard.

❤ RESPONSE

Have kids sit in a circle. Ask: **Was the challenge easier to accomplish with everyone participating or with just a few? Why? What would've happened if half the group had suddenly let go?**

Read aloud Acts 2:46-47.

Say: **Cooperation is like pulling on this rope as a team. As long as we each keep pulling, we're all safe. But if someone lets go, someone else might fall.**

Ask: **How do you cooperate at home? school? church? What could you do to start "pulling" for your friends more?**

❤ CLOSING

Have kids hold hands in a circle.

Pray: **Dear God, thanks for all the children in our church. Help us to see we can do more when we work together than we can do separately. In Jesus' name, amen.**

Welcome, Wanderer

By Dean Feldmeyer

● **Theme:** Hospitality
● **Scripture:** Hebrews 13:2
● **Overview:** Children join in a greeting game to learn the importance of hospitality.
● **Preparation:** You'll need a Bible.

● EXPERIENCE

Stand at the door and welcome kids as they enter the room. As you greet them, have them each line up beside you and join you in welcoming everyone else who comes. When everyone has arrived, have children sit down.

● RESPONSE

Say: **Throughout the Bible, we're constantly told to be kind to strangers and welcome them. Hebrews 13:2 is just one example of this kind of hospitality.**

Read aloud Hebrews 13:2.

Ask: **Why is it important to greet and welcome strangers? Why should we also welcome each other often? How does it feel to welcome others? How does it feel to be welcomed?**

● CLOSING

Pray: **Thank you, God, for welcoming us into your kingdom. Make us willing to welcome others who need you. In Jesus' name, amen.**

Wonderful Witnesses

By Jolene Roehlkepartain

Theme: Witnessing

Scripture: Hebrews 12:1-2

Overview: Kids see how people in the Bible were witnesses—and how they too can be witnesses for Jesus.

Preparation: For each pair you'll need a Bible. You'll need construction paper, a pencil, a basket, scissors, a large piece of white butcher paper and clear tape. Photocopy and cut apart the "Bible Pairs" handout (page 61). Make enough copies so each person can have one Bible character. Cut construction paper into cloud shapes. On each cloud shape, tape a Bible pair. Cut each cloud in half between the two names in a zigzag, curve or pattern—no two exactly alike. Cut out a large cloud from the piece of white butcher paper.

EXPERIENCE

Mix all the Bible character names in a basket and have children each draw one name and try to find the other half of their cloud. When kids each have found their partner, give pairs each a Bible and have them read the Bible passage on their cloud. Ask pairs each what their characters have in common.

RESPONSE

Read aloud Hebrews 12:1-2.

Say: **The people listed on your cloud make up a cloud of witnesses, and so do we.**

Tape the butcher-paper cloud to the wall. Have children each sign their name on the cloud.

Ask: **How does it feel to be one of God's witnesses? How can you be a good witness?**

CLOSING

Have kids each tape their Bible character's name from the construction paper to the cloud. Then have kids gather around the cloud. Have everyone look at the cloud while you pray: **God, thanks for the cloud of witnesses that you've given us. Help us to be good witnesses for you. In Jesus' name, amen.**

Bible Pairs

Adam Genesis	Eve 3:20
Abraham Genesis	Sarah 17:15-16
Isaac Genesis	Rebekah 24:66-67
Jacob Genesis	Rachel 29:28
Moses Exodus	Aaron 4:29-30
Naomi Ruth	Ruth 1:22
David 1 Samuel	Jonathan 18:1
Mary Matthew	Joseph 1:18
Peter Acts	John 4:1-4
Paul Acts	Barnabas 15:12

🍎 Back-to-School Blues

By Cindy Hansen

🍎 **Theme:** School worries

🍎 **Scripture:** Psalm 46:1-3

🍎 **Overview:** Children write problems and find solutions that show them how God helps them through back-to-school blues.

🍎 **Preparation:** For each person you'll need a piece of paper and a pencil. You'll also need a Bible, chalkboard and chalk.

🍎 EXPERIENCE

Give children each a piece of paper and a pencil. Form two groups. Have children in one group each write a problem they foresee in the upcoming school year. For example: "How am I going to get good grades?" "What do I do if somebody picks on me?" and "What if my best friend decides not to be my best friend anymore?"

Have children in the other group write advice on any problem they foresee in the upcoming school year. For example: "Always do your homework"; "Ask your parents to help"; and "Save money because you'll never know when you'll need some."

Have the problem-writers stand shoulder to shoulder in a line. Then have the solution-writers each stand facing a different problem-writer. Go down the line and have each problem-writer read a problem. Then have the solution-writer facing him or her read a solution. Solutions will be mixed up and zany, giving children lots of laughs.

🍎 RESPONSE

Form pairs by having children each get with the person facing them. Have partners each discuss one of the problems that most concerns them and brainstorm possible solutions. Have pairs each share their problems and possible solutions with the group. Write the problems and solutions on the chalkboard.

🍎 CLOSING

Read aloud Psalm 46:1-3 and add a modern version of verses 2 and 3 to the passage by adding the kids' concerns listed on the chalkboard. For example, "So I will not be afraid even though school begins soon, though I face tough problems, though I am alone and not invited to a party . . . "

Say: **God will help us. He asks us to give him our worries because he cares about us. God will help us through our back-to-school blues.**

Quick Devotions on
IMPORTANT FAITH
SUBJECTS

❖ *Believe It or Not!*

By Chris Yount

❖ **Theme:** Faith

❖ **Scripture:** Hebrews 11:1

❖ **Overview:** Children say whether they believe something that seems impossible—only to find that it's true.

❖ **Preparation:** For each person you'll need a small package of roasted peanuts. You'll also need an unshelled peanut hidden in your pocket and a Bible.

❖ EXPERIENCE

Say: **I have something in my pocket that no one has ever seen or touched.**

Ask: **Do you believe me? Why or why not?**

After kids respond, point out that kids' faith in your statement is based mostly on how well they know and trust you.

❖ RESPONSE

Take the peanut from your pocket and crack the shell. Show kids the shelled peanut. Read aloud Hebrews 11:1. Say: **Sometimes things in the Bible seem impossible. But the better we know God, the more we'll trust and believe what he says.**

Ask: **How can we know God better? How can we increase our faith that what he says is true?**

❖ CLOSING

Pray: **God, help us to know you better. Help us to see how trustworthy you are and believe what you say. In Jesus' name, amen.**

Give kids each a package of roasted peanuts as a reminder to get to know God better and trust what he says.

Clean and Everlasting

By Terry Vermillion

❖ **Theme:** Forgiveness

❖ **Scripture:** Titus 3:3-8

❖ **Overview:** Children remove color from Christmas ornaments and discuss how God can make us new.

❖ **Preparation:** For each person you'll need one round, glass Christmas tree ornament (the kind with a metal top and the color on the inside of the glass ball), about 1/2 cup of sand on a paper plate and a twig of plastic evergreen that can fit through the top of the ornament. You'll need a Bible. Provide extra adult supervision for the Experience section.

❖ EXPERIENCE

Have kids form a circle. Give each person a glass ornament and a sand-filled paper plate. Help kids each remove the metal top from their ornament and fill the ornament about half full of sand by rolling up their paper plate into a funnel. Then have kids each gently shake their ornament so that the sand swishes around inside and removes the color.

As kids work, ask: **What are some sins you've committed this week? How is this activity like the way God works in you to remove those sins from your life?**

❖ RESPONSE

When the ornaments are clear, have kids each dump their sand on their plate. Read aloud Titus 3:3-8. Give kids each a piece of evergreen and have them put it in their ornament. Then have kids each replace their metal top.

Say: **When you become a Christian, God changes you like you've changed the ornaments. He forgives your sins and gives you a new and everlasting life.**

❖ *CLOSING*

Have kids each hold up their ornament and look at it while you pray: **Dear God, thanks for removing the mistakes we've made. Thanks for forgiving our sins and giving us fresh, new life—like the evergreen. Help us follow your way. In Jesus' name, amen.**

Let kids each take their ornament home as a reminder of God's forgiveness.

Forever

By Kim Egolf-Fox

❖ **Theme:** God's love

❖ **Scripture:** 1 Corinthians 13:1-7

❖ **Overview:** Children stand in a circle and discuss where the circle begins and ends, then discuss how God's love never ends.

❖ **Preparation:** You'll need a few circular items such as a ring, a drawing of a circle, or a lid. You'll also need a Bible.

❖ EXPERIENCE

Have kids stand in as perfect a circle as possible. Stand in the center of the circle and examine the circle's shape. Reposition any members who appear out of the line of the circle.

Ask: **Where does this circle begin? Where does it end?**

Show children the other circular items you have and ask the same questions. Have kids remain standing while you read a Bible passage about something else that doesn't end. Read aloud 1 Corinthians 13:1-7.

❖ RESPONSE

Say: **The love spoken of in this passage is agape love, God's love. Jesus showed this love to others. It's a love that never ends.**

Ask: **How does knowing God loves you with a never-ending love help you? Knowing God loves you in this way, what should your love toward others be like?**

❖ CLOSING

Have children repeat this prayer line by line after you:

Dear God, you love us with a love that's like a circle,
a love with no beginning and no end,
a love that lasts forever.
Thank you for your very special love.
In Jesus' name, amen.

❖ *Got a Light?*

By Scott McKee

❖ *Theme:* Bible

❖ *Scripture:* Psalm 119:105

❖ *Overview:* Children complete an obstacle course in the dark using a flashlight, then see how the Bible is a "light" that helps them avoid danger.

❖ *Preparation:* Set up a simple obstacle course in a dark room. Include cardboard boxes, chairs or other large obstacles. For each group of four you'll need a flashlight. You'll also need a Bible, stereo equipment and a copy of Amy Grant's *Age to Age* album (Word) or something similar.

❖ EXPERIENCE

Form groups of four and give each group a flashlight. Lead children to the dark room and have groups each complete the obstacle course one at a time. Don't allow groups to watch each other complete the course.

❖ RESPONSE

Gather kids together and ask: **How did the flashlight help you complete the course? What would've happened if you didn't have the flashlight?**

Read aloud Psalm 119:105.

Ask: **How is the Bible like a light in our lives?**

❖ CLOSING

Say: **Just as a flashlight helps us see obstacles and avoid falling, the Bible helps us see dangers in our lives and avoid making mistakes. And like a flashlight, the Bible is no good unless it's used.**

Sing or listen to "Thy Word" from Amy Grant's *Age to Age* album or something similar.

 In The Bag

By Janet Kageler

❖ **Theme:** God's knowledge
❖ **Scripture:** Psalms 139:1-4
❖ **Overview:** Children try to remember what's in a bag, then discuss how God knows everything.
❖ **Preparation:** For each person you'll need a piece of paper and a pencil. You'll need a paper bag containing about 15 small items from your home or office; for example, paper clips, pens, rulers, pennies and junk mail. You'll also need a Bible.

❖ EXPERIENCE

Give kids each a piece of paper and a pencil. Show children the paper bag and ask them each to identify what's in it after you shake it two or three times. Then pour the contents out and let children look at the contents for 20 seconds. Put the contents back in the bag and have kids each list the items they remember.

❖ RESPONSE

Take a poll to see who remembered the most items.

Ask: **Do you know anyone who could've identified everything in the bag without looking?**

Read aloud Psalm 139:1-4. Based on the passage, have kids each list the things God knows.

Ask: **What are some other examples of things God knows that people don't know?**

❖ CLOSING

Say: **It's good that God knows everything, because that means he knows the best way to take care of each of us.**

Pray: **Thank you, God, that you know everything. Thank you that you know all our needs and how to care for each one of us. In Jesus' name, amen.**

❖ Jumping Psalms

By Sue McCallum

❖ **Theme:** Praise

❖ **Scripture:** Psalm 8:1; Psalm 18:2-3; and Psalm 66:3-4

❖ **Overview:** Children rewrite a Psalm into a jingle, then jump rope to it.

❖ **Preparation:** For each group of four you'll need a Bible, a piece of paper, a pencil and a jump-rope. Rewrite one of the passages below as a jingle kids can jump rope to. Use it as an example to show kids in the Experience section.

❖ EXPERIENCE

Form groups of four or fewer. Give groups each a Bible, a piece of paper and a pencil. Assign each group one of these Bible passages: Psalm 8:1; Psalm 18:2-3; or Psalm 66:3-4. Help groups each rewrite their Psalm into a jump-rope jingle.

❖ RESPONSE

Give groups each a jump-rope and have them each jump rope together and perform their jingles.

After applauding groups' efforts, ask: **Why is it good to praise God? How can we praise God? What's something about God you like to praise?**

❖ CLOSING

Have children kneel in a circle. Have groups each read aloud their jingle in turn as a closing prayer. After every group has read, say: **In Jesus' name, amen.**

❖ *Just a Little Kid*

By Dean Feldmeyer

❖ **Theme:** Serving God

❖ **Scripture:** 1 Samuel 3:1-10

❖ **Overview:** Kids compare baby food and adult food, then discuss ways children can serve God.

❖ **Preparation:** For each person you'll need a spoon and an apple slice. You'll also need a jar of strained applesauce for babies and a Bible.

❖ EXPERIENCE

Offer children each a taste of the strained applesauce. Then ask them to describe its taste and texture. Then give kids each an apple slice. Have them each compare the taste and texture of the apple to that of the baby food.

❖ RESPONSE

Ask: **What makes baby food appropriate for babies? What makes other foods appropriate for older people?**

Say: **Just as apples can be prepared in different ways for different age groups, so God's work can be done by people of all ages.**

Read aloud 1 Samuel 3:1-10

Say: **Samuel wasn't very old when he started doing God's work. He knew God doesn't call only adults to work for him. God calls kids too.**

Ask: **What kinds of work might God be calling you to do? What's one way you can start serving God this week?**

❖ CLOSING

Pray: **God, forgive us when we make excuses for not doing your work—excuses such as "I'm just a kid." Help us find and do the kind of work that's right for us. In Jesus' name, amen.**

❖Love Uniform

By Linda Snyder

❖ **Theme:** Christian love

❖ **Scripture:** John 13:35

❖ **Overview:** Children play a guessing game to determine a person's job, and learn that love is the job of a Christian.

❖ **Preparation:** For each person you'll need a construction paper heart and a straight pin. You'll also need a Bible. Collect symbols that identify various occupations; for example, a stethoscope, police badge, firefighter's hat, rolling pin, and nurse's cap.

❖ EXPERIENCE

Have kids form a circle. Say: **We're going to play Who Am I? Many jobs have a uniform or specific equipment that makes them easy to recognize. When I hold up the clue, tell me who you think I am.**

Hold up the job symbols one at a time and let children guess the jobs.

❖ RESPONSE

After children have guessed all the symbols, ask: **How did you know who I was? What other jobs have symbols that make them easy to pick out? What do you think the job symbol for a Christian would be?**

Read aloud John 13:35.

Ask: **How can people tell that we're Christians? What uniform do we wear?**

❖ CLOSING

Pin a construction paper heart on each person's shirt. Pray: **Dear God, help us remember that our Christian uniform is love. Help us let our love show—just like the paper hearts we're wearing. In Jesus' name, amen.**

❖Making God Happy

By Mike Gillespie

❖ **Theme:** God's love

❖ **Scripture:** John 3:16

❖ **Overview:** Children form candy hearts and focus on ways they make God proud.

❖ **Preparation:** For each person you'll need construction paper, glue and a pencil. You'll also need a bag of candy hearts and a Bible.

❖ EXPERIENCE

Give children each a piece of construction paper, glue and a pencil. Hand kids each enough candy hearts for them each to make a large heart shape on the construction paper. Have children each glue their candy hearts in place.

Say: **God loves us very much. What is there about you that makes God happy? For example, you might say, "I like to be nice to everyone." Think of three specific things and write them inside your heart.**

While kids write, read aloud John 3:16.

❖ RESPONSE

Ask: **Why did God want Jesus to come and help us? When have you loved someone so much you did something brave to show it? If you were God, what would you do to show people how much you love them?**

❖ CLOSING

Let children each share what they wrote in their heart. Vote as a group on the one item on each list that best fits that person. Pray: **Dear God, thank you for loving us. Help us be the best Christians we can be. Thank you for sending us Jesus. In Jesus' name, amen.**

Have the kids each take home their heart as a reminder of God's love.

❖ *Mirror Images*

By Janet Kageler

❖ **Theme:** Bible study

❖ **Scripture:** James 1:23-25

❖ **Overview:** Children try to draw themselves from memory to show how they need to read the Bible to discover who they are.

❖ **Preparation:** For each person you'll need a piece of paper and a marker. You'll also need a mirror and a Bible.

❖ EXPERIENCE

Give children each a piece of paper and a marker. Allow 10 seconds for kids each to look at themselves in a mirror. Then have them each draw a self-portrait from memory.

When everyone has finished, pass the mirror around and have kids grade themselves—A, B or C—on how close their self-portrait matches their mirror image.

Ask: **How high was your grade? Why? Why was it hard to draw your self-portrait? What would've made it easier?**

❖ RESPONSE

Read aloud James 1:23-25.

Say: **The more you look into a mirror, the better your self-portrait will be. And the more you look into the Bible, the better you can do what it says.**

❖ CLOSING

Challenge children each to read in their Bible on four different days in the coming week. Suggest they read two to four verses from James 1 at each sitting and then write one thing they learn from each reading.

Pray: **Lord, we know you want us to study and learn from the Bible. Help us spend time reading our Bibles this week. In Jesus' name, amen.**

❖Paint a Prayer

By Terry Vermillion

❖ **Theme:** Prayer

❖ **Scripture:** Matthew 6:9-13

❖ **Overview:** Kids paint symbols to represent parts of the Lord's Prayer, then discuss prayer's importance.

❖ **Preparation:** For each person you'll need a sheet of newsprint and a paintbrush. For every two or three people you'll need a jar of water and a box of watercolors. You'll also need a Bible.

❖ EXPERIENCE

Give children each newsprint and a paintbrush. Give every two or three people a jar of water and a box of watercolors. Have children each paint six sections on their newsprint. Read aloud Matthew 6:9-13. After you read each verse, pause and have kids paint a picture or symbol of the verse in one section. Offer suggestions. For example, "We pray that your kingdom will come" might be represented by a castle or a flag.

❖ RESPONSE

Have kids explain their paintings. Ask: **Why should we pray? What things do you pray about? How do your prayers help you?**

❖ CLOSING

Have children stand in a circle. Pray aloud Matthew 6:9-13 while kids each look at the symbols they made.

❖ *Paper-Clip Churches*

By Linda Snyder

❖ *Theme:* Church

❖ *Scripture:* Colossians 3:19

❖ *Overview:* Children use paper clips to explore characteristics of the church.

❖ *Preparation:* For each person you'll need 20 paper clips. You'll also need a Bible.

❖ EXPERIENCE

Give each person 20 paper clips. Have kids each make a paper-clip chain.

Ask: **Why are paper-clip chains more fun than just one paper clip by itself?**

Say: **The church is a lot like a paper-clip chain. We're linked together by our faith. And no matter how long a paper-clip chain gets, there's always room for more. Churches should also be ready to grow because Jesus commands us to share Jesus with others.**

Have kids each connect their chains together, forming one long chain.

❖ RESPONSE

Ask: **In what other ways is the church like a paper-clip chain?**

After kids respond, read aloud Colossians 3:19.

Say: **The church was built to work like a body.**

Ask: **What makes a church strong today? How do churches grow?**

❖ CLOSING

Form two teams and have a tug of war with the paper-clip chain. Note the strength of the paper clips when they're connected.

Pray: **Dear Lord, help us understand that churches are strong when people worship together and share their faith. Thank you for giving us each other to help us grow.**

After prayer, divide the paper-clip chain into 20-paper-clip segments. Have kids each take home a small chain as a reminder of the strength of God's church.

❖ *Rock Solid*

By Mike Gillespie

❖ ***Theme:*** Faith and the church

❖ ***Scripture:*** Matthew 16:18

❖ ***Overview:*** Children compare themselves with rocks as the foundation for God's church.

❖ ***Preparation:*** For each person you'll need a smooth fist-size rock, a small paintbrush and a small sheet of newsprint. You'll also need several colors of Tempra paint—each poured into a jar—and a Bible

❖ EXPERIENCE

Have kids sit in a circle with the rocks, paintbrushes, paint and newsprint in the center. Have kids each get a rock and a sheet of newsprint, and paint the words "God's church" on their newsprint.

Read aloud Matthew 16:18.

Say: **God chose to build his church on the foundation of Peter's faith. We share in that faith as part of God's church.**

❖ RESPONSE

Have children each paint their name on their rock.

Ask: **How can you help God build his kingdom in you? How can you help build God's church?**

❖ CLOSING

Have kids each place their rock in the center of the circle.

Pray: **Dear God, help us to be a rock like Peter. Help us to have faith in you. In Jesus' name, amen.**

Have children each take home their rock as a reminder to follow God in faith.

❖ *Tearing Temptation*

By Mike Gillespie

❖ **Theme:** Overcoming temptation

❖ **Scripture:** Matthew 4:1-11

❖ **Overview:** Children list temptations they face, then tear their list to show how Jesus helps them overcome temptation.

❖ **Preparation:** For each person you'll need a marker. You'll also need a 10- to 15-foot sheet of newsprint, tape and a Bible. Divide the paper into three sections labeled "School," "Friends" or "Family."

❖ EXPERIENCE

Lay the newsprint on the floor in the center of the room. Form three groups, and give kids each a marker. Have groups each work around a different section of the newsprint, writing temptations they face in that area of life. For example: "I'm sometimes tempted at school to cheat on a test"; "I'm sometimes tempted to gossip about my friends"; or "I'm sometimes tempted to lie to my family members." When children are finished, tape the newsprint to the wall and have groups share what they wrote.

❖ RESPONSE

Read aloud Matthew 4:1-11.

Ask: **What did Jesus learn about temptation? Why could he say no to temptation? When have you said no to temptation? When have you said yes?**

Say: **Jesus came to give us the courage to say no to temptation. We can break free from it because of what Christ did on the cross.**

❖ CLOSING

Say: **With Jesus in our hearts, we can tear through the power of temptation and say no to sin.**

Have children tear the newsprint off the wall, rip it

into pieces and have a fun paper-wad fight to show how Jesus enables them to destroy temptation's power.

❖ *The Birth of Laughter*

By Ed McNulty

❖ **Theme:** God's power

❖ **Scripture:** Genesis 17:15-17 and 21:1-6

❖ **Overview:** Children try to do and imagine impossible tasks to see that anything is possible with God.

❖ **Preparation:** You'll need a Bible.

❖ EXPERIENCE

Tell kids to jump up and touch the ceiling. After a couple of tries, have children take off their shoes and imagine an elephant putting them on.

Say: **Impossible? Silly? Then you can imagine how a 90-year-old woman and a 100-year-old man felt when God told them something impossible was about to happen.**

Read aloud Genesis 17:15-17.

❖ RESPONSE

Ask children how God might help in the first two "impossible" situations you mentioned. For example, God might send an angel to boost kids to the ceiling. Or God might shrink the elephant's feet to fit into kids' shoes.

Ask: **What's something God can help you do that's hard for you to do alone?**

Say: **When God told Abraham and Sarah they were going to have a baby, Abraham laughed. He thought having a baby at his age was a crazy idea, because he was very old. But Sarah had a baby boy. And they named him Isaac, which in Hebrew means "laughter" or "he laughs."**

Read aloud Genesis 21:1-6.

❖ CLOSING

Have kids close their eyes and reach their hands into the air as you pray aloud: **Dear God, all things are possible with you. Help us always believe in your power no** matter how impossible situations may seem. In Jesus' name, amen.

❖ The Chain Gang

By Carol Younger

❖ **Theme:** Sin

❖ **Scripture:** John 8:34-36

❖ **Overview:** Children wrap themselves in paper chains and experience how their sins tie them down.

❖ **Preparation:** For each person you'll need several strips of construction paper, a pencil and a stapler. You'll also need a Bible.

❖ EXPERIENCE

Give kids each several strips of construction paper and a pencil. On each strip have them each write one sin they've committed in the last week. Have children each staple the ends of one of their paper strips together—creating a loop. Then have them take another strip, put it through the first loop and staple the ends together. Have children continue until they've each created a chain. When the chains are complete, have each put their chain around their neck. Then have them each share one sin they wrote on their chain.

❖ RESPONSE

Ask: **What would it be like if we couldn't take off these chains and had to wear them all the time? What would our lives be like if we could never let go of the things we do wrong?**

Read aloud John 8:34-36 and have kids take off each other's chains.

Ask: **How does Jesus help us get rid of our chains? What can we do to help him help us?**

❖ CLOSING

Have children each remove one link from their chain and take it home as a reminder of God's forgiveness. Then have kids each rip through their chain to symbolically show how God frees them from their sin.

Pray: **Thank you, God, for forgiving us. Help us give you all our sins, so they won't tie us down. In Jesus' name, amen.**

❖ *Tight Ropes*

By Bob Hicks

❖ **Theme:** Faith

❖ **Scripture:** James 2:14-17

❖ **Overview:** Children walk across a tightrope placed on a floor as a challenge to put their faith into action.

❖ **Preparation:** For each person you'll need a 1-foot string. You'll also need a 20-foot rope and a Bible.

❖ EXPERIENCE

Lay the rope straight on the floor and ask kids each to pretend it's hanging high above the Grand Canyon. Have kids each walk the length of the tightrope. When everyone has gone, have two adults hold the rope tight about five feet off the floor. Ask for volunteers to walk across the tightrope now. If anyone volunteers, keep up the bluff until it becomes unsafe. The children will usually back down once they try to get up to the rope's height.

❖ RESPONSE

Have children sit in a circle.

Ask: **Why was everybody willing to walk across the tightrope the first time? Why was the second time different? How is this tightrope like our faith in God?**

Read aloud James 2:14-17.

Say: **Believing in Jesus is easy until he asks us to do something for him. But if we believe in Christ, we'll be committed to do what he says to do.**

❖ CLOSING

Give children each a string to remind them to put their faith into action. Close with prayer, asking God to give kids the courage to live out what they believe.

❖ What God Wants

By Carol Younger

❖ **Theme:** Pleasing God
❖ **Scripture:** Micah 6:8
❖ **Overview:** Kids learn what pleases God by trying to make a king smile.
❖ **Preparation:** You'll need a Bible. Choose one person to be the "king." Tell the king that he or she may not smile except when kids communicate words or actions that deal with treating people fairly, helping others, being kind or spending time with God.

❖ EXPERIENCE

Have the king sit on a chair (the throne) with a somber face, and introduce him or her to the kids. Form teams of four or fewer, and have teams each come before the king and do or say something to make the king smile. Give each team only one chance to make the king smile.

❖ RESPONSE

Decide as a group what things did or didn't make the king happy. Have the king tell the group what he or she was waiting for.

Ask: **What things do you think please God?**

Read aloud Micah 6:8. Have children compare what they think God wants from them with what this verse says God requires.

❖ CLOSING

Pray: **God, sometimes we don't do what you really want us to do. Sometimes we forget about taking care of the people who're left out. Sometimes we forget how much you want to spend time with us. Help us learn to give you the things you really want from us. In Jesus' name, amen.**

❖ Give a Little Christmas

By Cindy Hansen

❖ **Theme:** Giving at Christmas

❖ **Scripture:** Genesis 13:15-16; Luke 2:10-11; John 10:27-28; 14:16-17; and Galatians 1:4-5

❖ **Overview:** Kids make an ornament and a gift certificate to give away, then reflect on how much God has given us.

❖ **Preparation:** For each person you'll need a paper clip, a 4-inch circle of aluminum foil, scissors, a pencil and a copy of the "Christmas Gift Certificate" handout (page 90). You'll also need a Bible.

❖ EXPERIENCE

Say: **Christmas is a time for remembering God's greatest gift to us. He gave his son to die for us. Listen to other gifts God has given us.**

Help volunteers read aloud the scriptures about these gifts:

● Blessings—Genesis 13:15-16;
● Eternal life—John 10:27-28;
● The Holy Spirit—John 14:16-17; and
● Forgiveness—Galatians 1:4-5.

Say: **At Christmas we give to others because God has already given us so much. We're going to make a Christmas ornament and gift certificate for another person. You decide who to give it to.**

Give children each a paper clip, a circle of aluminum foil and scissors. Have kids cut the aluminum foil in a spiral, then reshape the paper clip to form a hook. Secure the hook on top of the foil spiral to complete the ornament.

❖ RESPONSE

When everyone is finished, have children each think of one thing they could do as a gift for another person; for example, take out the trash, vacuum the car, make breakfast, clean the house, help a friend with homework.

Give kids each a "Christmas Gift Certificate" handout and a pencil, and have them each write their gift idea on it. Then have kids each talk about their ideas with someone sitting close by.

❖ CLOSING

Close with this echo prayer. You say a line, then have kids repeat it.

Christmas is a time for giving.
Keep us, God, from ever forgetting
your gift of Jesus ever living.
We'll say we love you again and again.
Amen. Amen. Amen. Amen.

Let kids take home their ornaments. Encourage kids to give away their certificates to celebrate how much God has given us.

Foil Ornament

Christmas Gift Certificate

To: _____

My gift: _____

_____

_____

When I'll
give my gift: _____

Merry Christmas!
Signed, _____

Topical Index

Scripture Index

More Creative Programming Resources...

FIDGET BUSTERS

101 Quick Attention-Getters for Children's Ministry

Jolene L. Roehlkepartain

Teach children more—by keeping them focused on your lesson. Be ready whenever short attention spans give way to wiggles and squirms. Simply grab one of these quick activities—get kids up and moving—then bring them back to the lesson ready to learn!

You'll get lively, age-appropriate ideas that...

- require little or no preparation
- get kids excited about learning
- burn up excess energy
- help you take—and keep—control of your group

... as they perk up kids' interest... and keep them coming back to your class for more. Help your kids enjoy learning—and build closeness in your group—with these creative activities carefully planned for children from preschool through the sixth grade.

ISBN 1-55945-058-4 $8.99

5-MINUTE MESSAGES FOR CHILDREN

Donald Hinchey

Captivate and challenge young listeners—with 52 Bible-based sermons just for them. Each creative message uses language kids readily understand—so you'll teach meaningful lessons on Bible-based topics such as...

- God's love
- faith
- putting God first
- forgiveness

... and dozens of other topics. Plus, each talk uses involving activities to grab and hold kids' attention—so they'll remember the truths you present.

You'll also get seasonal ideas for helping children understand the meaning of...

- Advent
- Easter
- Pentecost
- Christmas

... and other important days. You'll use these lessons for children's moments in Sunday worship—or at camps, retreats and other special events.

ISBN 1-55945-030-4 $8.99

Available at your local Christian bookstore, or write: Group Books, Box 485, Loveland, CO 80539. Please add postage/handling of $3 for mail orders of up to $15, $4 for orders of $15.01+. Colorado residents add 3% sales tax.

Innovative Resources for Children's Ministry

CHILDREN'S MINISTRY CLIP ART

Mary Lynn Ulrich

Add pizazz and style to your ministry with **Children's Ministry Clip Art**. Use these lively illustrations in newsletters, fliers, letters and on bulletin boards—anywhere you need to grab kids'—and parents'—attention.

With this creative art, you can...

- design fabulous fliers and handouts for meetings on dozens of topics
- announce upcoming events with zany, attention-getting calendars
- promote specific children's ministry programs

This giant collection of clip art will add a professional touch to your children's ministry. It's as easy as 1-2-3.

1—Choose your art. 2—Cut it out. 3—Paste it down and your publicity is ready to go!

ISBN 1-55945-018-5 $14.99

UPPER-ELEMENTARY MEETINGS

Compiled by the editors of Group Books

Build faith in upper-elementary kids! You'll discover 20 well-planned meetings on a variety of topics—all designed specifically to build faith in upper-elementary kids. You'll save tons of planning time as you teach powerful Christian lessons such as...

- being a child of God
- helping the hungry
- what's great about parents
- God's will
- temptation
- what is faith?

All step-by-step meeting plans come complete with crowdbreakers, Bible studies and devotions. Plus, you'll cut preparation time with loads of creative handouts you can photocopy. Your kids will love the action built into each program. And you'll get solid help dealing with the tough issues they now face...

- divorce
- self-image
- peer pressure
- drugs
- sexuality

ISBN 0-931529-86-7 $12.99

FUN GROUP GAMES FOR CHILDREN'S MINISTRY

Get 100 faith-building games to energize activities with elementary kids. Discover exciting games to...

- increase Bible knowledge
- teach teamwork
- have fun!
- experience cooperation
- build group unity

You'll also find...

- Bible-learning games for communicating basic Bible knowledge
- energy-burning games for helping kids settle down
- games with a message for increasing kids' sensitivity toward others
- fun groups games for low- or no-competition activities everyone can play
- relays for wild variations of the ever-popular race
- teamwork-builders for helping kids learn to cooperate with one another

These 100 games provide endless options for use in Sunday school, meetings, parties, summer camps—wherever you have a group of kids.

ISBN 1-55945-003-7 $9.99

Add Fun and Creativity to Your Ministry...

CHILDREN'S MINISTRY THAT WORKS!

The Basics & Beyond

Build your children's program with this complete, practical handbook for working with kids from birth through grade six. You'll learn the secrets of successful children's ministry from over 20 children's ministry veterans. This useful handbook will become your one-stop source of creative ideas for ...

- Sunday school
- children's church
- vacation Bible school

... even after-school programs and ministries to special-needs children. Plus, you'll ease your workload with money-saving tips and ready-to-use work sheets.

ISBN 0-931529-69-7 $12.99

LIVELY BIBLE LESSONS

Make creative teaching a snap with 20 complete lessons for each age level. You'll find fun and meaningful activities to teach children ...

- why each one is a special person
- how God helps them with their fears
- how to be good friends
- who Jesus is—and what he did for them

... plus, plenty of creative lessons for special celebrations—Easter, birthdays, Thanksgiving and Christmas.

Preschoolers   ISBN 1-55945-067-3 $9.99
Grades K-3   ISBN 1-55945-074-6 $9.99